3. BMW Z8 2-door Convertible Roadster

BMW Motors is the great rival to Mercedes among German sports cars and performance luxury sedans. The company started as an airplane-engine builder in the early twentieth century, switched to motorcycles in 1923, and eventually added automobile production. BMW has since captured the respect and enthusiasm of discerning and demanding auto buyers.

Pictured is one of their low-production, high-performance sports cars,

the Z8. Built from 2000 to 2003, the 2-seat roadster (c⟮ equipped with a powerful 5-liter V-8 engine that develops 40⟮ 0-to-60 mph time of just 4.7 seconds and is governed to a top mph (capable of 180 mph without governor). The $134,00 had a production volume of only ten cars per week.

4. Porsche 911 GT2 Twin-turbo 2-door Coupe

The third rival to Mercedes in the German sports-car world is Porsche. Basing their production cars on a long history of racing-car victories, Porsche emphasizes performance and speed over luxury and comfort. The vehicle shown is a version of the famous 911 series, which began production in the 1960s. The 2003 911 GT2, however, is much different from earlier versions: the engine size and power have been increased over the years, among other improvements. The horizontally opposed 6-cylinder engine (called a "boxer" due to its box shape) produces a whopping 462 hp with its twin turbochargers. The rear-engined coupe can go from 0 to 60 in just 4.1 seconds and reach a top speed of 200 mph! A total of 300 vehicles was produced from 2001 to 2003. The 911 GT2 sold for $183,000.

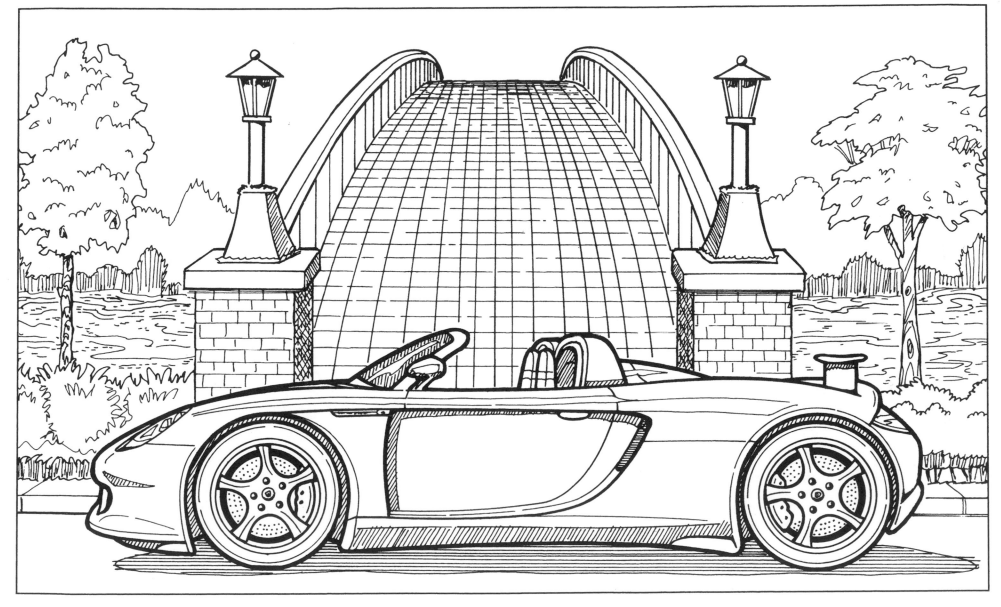

5. Porsche Carrera GT 2-door Coupe/Convertible

For 2004, Porsche introduced an exciting new vehicle type, the Carrera GT. A departure from Porsche's long-standing tradition of rear-engined sports cars, the Carrera GT features a mid-engine layout for maximum weight balance and distribution. Equipped with a 5.7-liter V-10 engine rated at 604 hp, the Carrera GT can hit 202 mph and has a 0-to-60 mph time of only 3.8 seconds. Its carbon-fiber body features a rear air spoiler that automatically raises and lowers depending on speed. At higher speeds, the spoiler creates an air down-force to increase rear traction. The vehicle sells in the $400,000 to $500,000 range.

6. Rolls-Royce Phantom 4-door Sedan

At the other end of the spectrum from maximum-performance-oriented Porsches are the vehicles that focus on the ultimate in luxury and opulence—the renowned Rolls-Royces. Since the early twentieth century, these English sedans have been virtually hand-built from the finest materials, with unsurpassable craftsmanship. The Rolls-Royce Flying Lady hood ornament automatically commands attention and respect for the most prestigious car in production.

Rolls-Royce's latest luxury sedan, the Phantom, was introduced in 2003. Equipped with every luxury option, including built-in telephone, television, and satellite computer navigation, the 6,000-lb. luxury cruiser can have any customer-desired feature designed and installed. The Phantom is no slow poke—with its 6.7-liter V-12 engine putting out 453 hp, the three-ton sedan can travel from 0 to 60 mph in 5.7 seconds and reach a top speed of 149 mph. The Phantom sells for $333,000.

7. Rolls-Royce Corniche 2-door Convertible

For those who prefer a dash of sportiness and fresh air with their luxury, Rolls-Royce also produces the Corniche convertible. Introduced in 2000, the beautifully detailed vehicle features all the standard luxury amenities and quality craftsmanship of the Rolls-Royce nameplate. With a 6.7-liter V-8 engine rated at 325 hp, the Corniche can reach 139 mph and has a 0-to-60 mph time of 8.5 seconds. The Corniche model is built to order for individual customers. It is priced in the $300,000 to $400,000 range.

8. Jaguar XJ220 2-door Coupe

Another English automobile brand that exudes luxury and performance is Jaguar. The company has had a long history of building luxurious sedans and race-winning sports cars. The beautiful, sleek Jaguar XJ220 coupe was produced from 1992 to 1994. Combining ultra-high performance with superb comfort and style, the XJ220 once held the title of world's fastest production car. With a twin-turbocharged 3.5-liter V-6 engine creating a powerful 543 hp, the XJ220 could reach an eye-popping top speed of 213 mph. It could sprint from 0-to-60 mph in 4 seconds, and 0-100 mph in a blinding 7.3 seconds. Within its three-year production run, only 275 XJ220s were built, at an astounding $705,000 each.

9. Aston Martin DB9 2-door Sports Coupe

This English sports car nameplate gained fame from its specially equipped model DB5, which was featured in the 1964 James Bond movie *Goldfinger*. Although current Aston Martins are very well equipped with performance and luxury options, they don't come standard with grille-mounted machine guns or passenger ejector seats!

The model pictured above is the DB9 sports coupe, introduced in 2003. With its handsome all-aluminum body, the sports coupe is built for high speed and quiet, luxurious cruising. The DB9 is powered by a 6-liter V-12 engine putting out a hefty 450 hp. The vehicle has a 0-to-60 mph time of 4.7 seconds and can attain a top speed of 186 mph. It is priced in the $150,000 range.

10. Aston Martin Vanquish 2-door Sports Coupe

A stablemate to the DB9 is the Aston Martin Vanquish. Built from 2001 to 2002, it could be ordered as either a two-seater or a two-plus-two (with smaller seats in the rear compartment). Its 6-liter V-12 engine, rated at 460 hp, gives the Vanquish a top speed of 190 mph and a 0-to-60 mph time of 4.6 seconds. Its production volume was only 200 vehicles for 2001, and 250 vehicles for 2002. The price tag for the Vanquish was in the $100,000 to $120,000 range.

11. Lamborghini Diablo 2-door Coupe

In 1966, Italian industrialist and automaker Ferruchio Lamborghini challenged the motoring world with the introduction of his stunningly crafted super-sports car, the Miura. Designed to compete with the best sports cars from rival Ferrari, the Miura became an instant classic. Since then, Lamborghini Motors has produced one great luxury/sports car after another.

The successful Lamborghini Diablo was sold from 1990 to 2001. The low-slung, super-sleek body of the vehicle, originally constructed of aluminum, was replaced by high-tech carbon-fiber material in 1999. The Diablo was powered by a 5.7 liter, 492 hp V-12 engine. In its initial year of production, the Diablo won the title of world's fastest production vehicle, with a top speed of 202 mph. The price tag for a Diablo was $270,000.

12. Lamborghini Murciélago 2-door Coupe

In 2002, Lamborghini introduced the successor to the Diablo, the Murciélago. With its carbon-fiber body and forward/upswinging "gull-wing" doors, the Murciélago is an immediate attention-getter. The power-plant of the new sports car was upgraded to a 6.2-liter V-12 producing a bruising 580 hp, with a top speed of 205 mph. Only 1,500 Murciélago models are slated for production, with a price of $250,000 each.

17. Bentley Arnage T-24 Mulliner 4-door Sedan

At the other end of the limited-edition production car range from the Ferraris are the models from British builder Bentley. These luxurious automobiles represent the utmost in comfort, style, quality, and deluxe features. With interiors covered in the finest leather and hand-crafted wood, the Bentley Arnage T-24 Mulliner competes with Rolls-Royce for the prestige automobile buyer's business. A large, heavy vehicle at 5,900 lbs., the Arnage T-24 is also powerful and fast. Its twin-turbocharged V-8 engine, producing 450 hp, can propel the vehicle to 168 mph and give it a 0-to-60 mph time of a scant 5.5 seconds. Introduced in 2004, the Bentley Arnage T-24 sells in the $300,000 to $400,000 range.

18. Bentley Azure Series 2-door Convertible

Shown here is the sporty yet elegant Bentley Azure Series convertible. Built with the same superb-quality materials and craftsmanship as the more stately sedan models, the 2-door open-air vehicle was built from 2003 to 2004 in a very limited edition of just 24 cars. The Bentley convertible is powered by a 400 hp turbocharged V-8 engine which can propel the 5,000-lb. car from 0-to-60 in 6.5 seconds, with a top speed of 155 mph. These stylish vehicles have a selling price of $370,000.

19. Bentley Continental GT 2-door Coupe

In 2004, Bentley introduced a new model, the GT coupe. With a smooth, rakish body design, this new Bentley has all the makings of an instant classic. The GT coupe has the full complement of luxury accessories combined with outstanding power and performance. Its twin-turbocharged 6-liter V-12 engine produces a mighty 552 hp, enabling the GT to reach a top speed of 186 mph, with a 0-to-60 mph time of only 4.7 seconds. The sleek and powerful Bentley GT sells in the $150,000 range.

20. Maserati Spyder 2-door Convertible/Roadster

Maserati is another great nameplate in Italian sports/luxury cars. Shown above is a Spyder convertible brought out by Maserati in 2003. Fast and luxurious, the Spyder is powered by a 4.2 liter V-8 engine churning out a whopping 415 hp. With its lightweight convertible body, the Spyder has a top speed of 177 mph and a 0-to-60 time of 4.9 seconds. One of the least expensive Italian sports/luxury vehicles, it sells in the $100,000 range.

21. Dodge Viper SRT-10 Convertible/Coupe

The American-built Dodge Viper 2-seat sports car, both coupe and convertible, has been in production since 1991. By 2002, over 15,000 Vipers had been built. During that time, its engine size and power have increased dramatically—from an initial V-10 engine of 8.1-liters/400 hp, to an 8.3-liter/550 hp V-10 for the 2003 Viper SRT-10 model. This latest version can achieve 60 mph in a lightning-quick 3.9 seconds and reach a top speed of 198 mph. Even though the Viper has a full array of luxury features, it is the lowest-priced vehicle among the super-luxurious cars shown in this book. A new Viper can be acquired for the relatively bargain-basement price of $84,000.

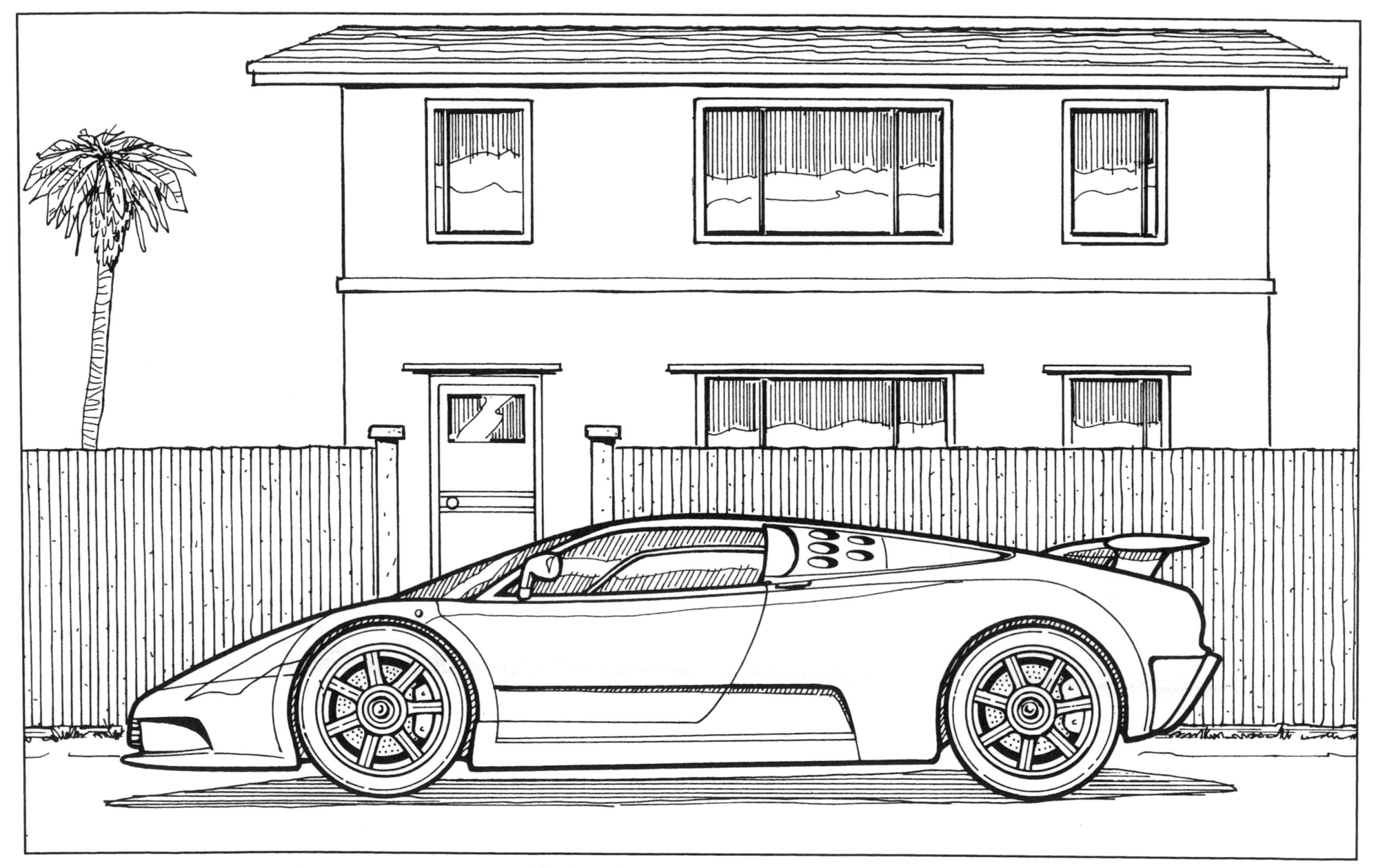

22. Bugatti EB 110S 2-door Coupe

A rare and very expensive sports/luxury automobile was introduced by Bugatti Motors in 1991. To celebrate the 110th birthday of the company's founder, Ettore Bugatti, the manufacturer built the EB110S. Incredibly eye-catching and stylish, the beautiful speedster could reach 212 mph at the top end and had a 0-to-60 time of 4.4 seconds. It was powered by a 560 hp, 3.5-liter V-12 engine with *four* turbochargers. Built from 1991 to 1995, only 24 EB110S models were produced, with a selling price of $350,000 each.

23. McClaren F1 2-door Coupe

This vehicle, essentially a Grand Prix race car modified for street production, held the title of world's fastest production car for a number of years. Designed and produced from 1993 to 1997 by the McLaren racing division of Mercedes-Benz, the F1 has an official top speed of 231 mph. The power for that speed is supplied by a 6.1-liter V-12 engine pumping out an amazing 627 hp. It can hit 60 mph in the blink of an eye—just 3.2 seconds. Constructed of carbon fiber and aluminum, only 100 of these cars were built, with a stupendous sticker price of $810,000.

24. Saleen S7 2-door Coupe

Just when you think you've seen the slickest-looking sports/luxury vehicle around, another one comes along—such is the case with the 2000 Saleen S7. With its incredibly low roof-line and plentiful array of engine-cooling air scoops, it seems to be traveling at 200 mph just sitting in the parking lot! This American-built car has a mammoth 7-liter Ford V-8 engine tuned to produce 550 hp. The carbon-fiber–bodied speed demon has been track-tested at 220 mph; it sells in the $400,000 range.

27. Vector W8-M12 2-door Coupe

Another sensational sports/luxury car design is the Italian-American–built Vector W8-M12. With gorgeous flowing body lines highlighted by the impressive rear spoiler, it is a work of art in aluminum and carbon fiber. Built from 1992 to 1997, the Vector was originally equipped with a small-block, twin-turbocharged Chevy V-8 engine, tuned to deliver a staggering 1,100 hp. In this configuration the Vector had a top speed of 218 mph and a 0-to-60 time of 4 seconds. In 1994, Vector was bought by another automaker, and the W8 was refitted with a 5.7-liter Lamborghini V-12 engine producing 492 hp. Its performance was lowered slightly to 190 mph and 4.8 seconds. The Vector's selling price was a substantial $185,000.

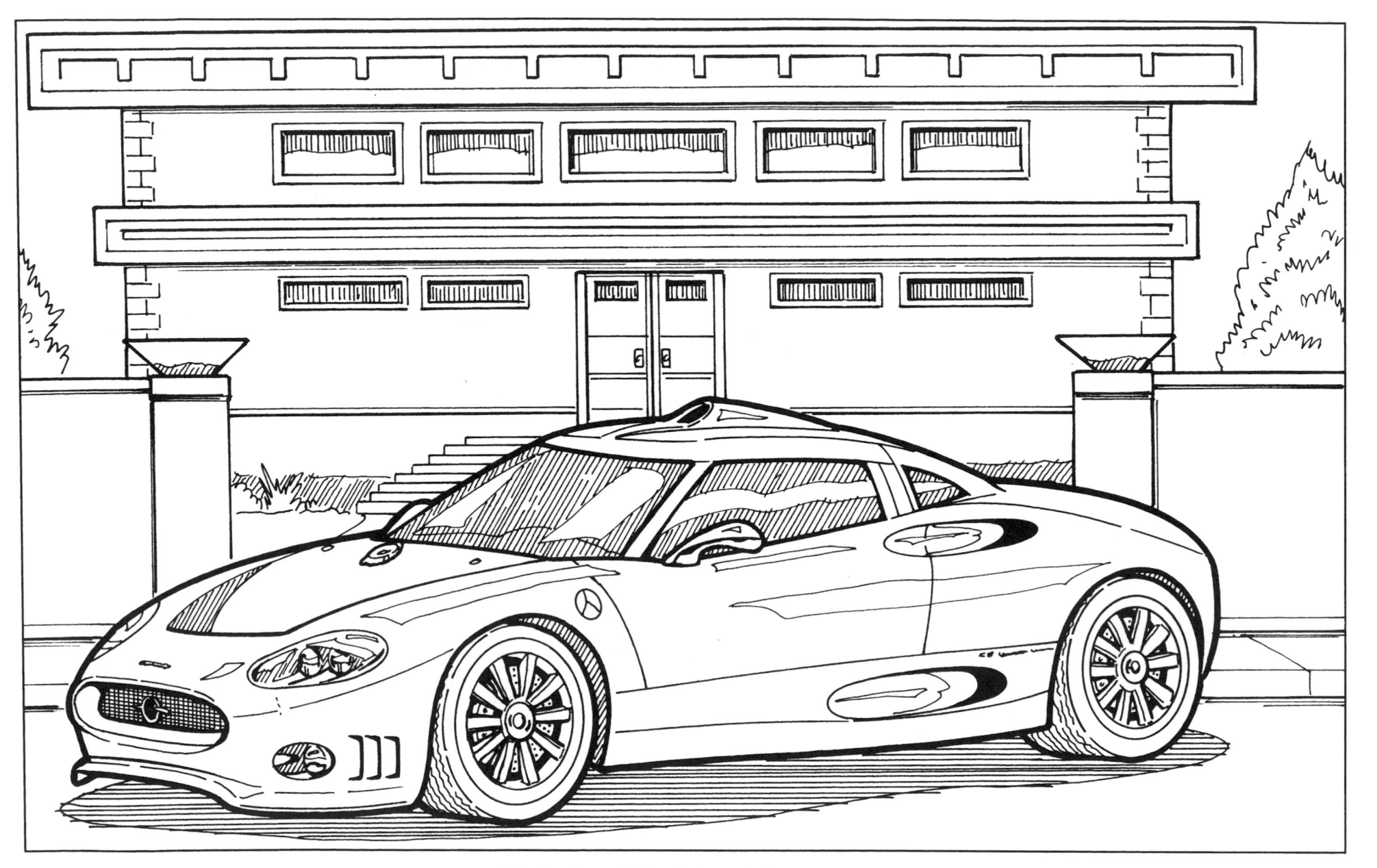

28. Spyker C8 Laviolette 2-door Coupe

The exotic Spyker C8 coupe, built in the Netherlands, was introduced in 2001. The name "Laviolette" was given to the car in honor of Valentin Laviolette, one of the company's founders in the early 1900s. With its unique roof-mounted air scoop to aid in cooling the mid-engine layout, the C8 weighs only 2,589 lbs.—even with a full array of luxury features. Coupled with a 4.2-liter Audi V-8 engine of 450 hp, the coupe can reach a top speed of 186 mph and has a 0-to-60 mph time of 4.4 seconds.

29. Ford GT 2-door Coupe

This new Ford GT sports/luxury vehicle was introduced as a production car in late 2003. Based on the famous Ford GT 40 racing cars that won the 1966 24-hour Le Mans race in first, second, and third place, it has become another instant classic for well-heeled auto enthusiasts. The GT is powered by a 5.4-liter Ford V-8 engine delivering a considerable 500 hp. The low-slung speedster can reach 198 mph and travel from 0-to-60 in just 3.6 seconds. The new Ford GT has a selling price of $145,000.

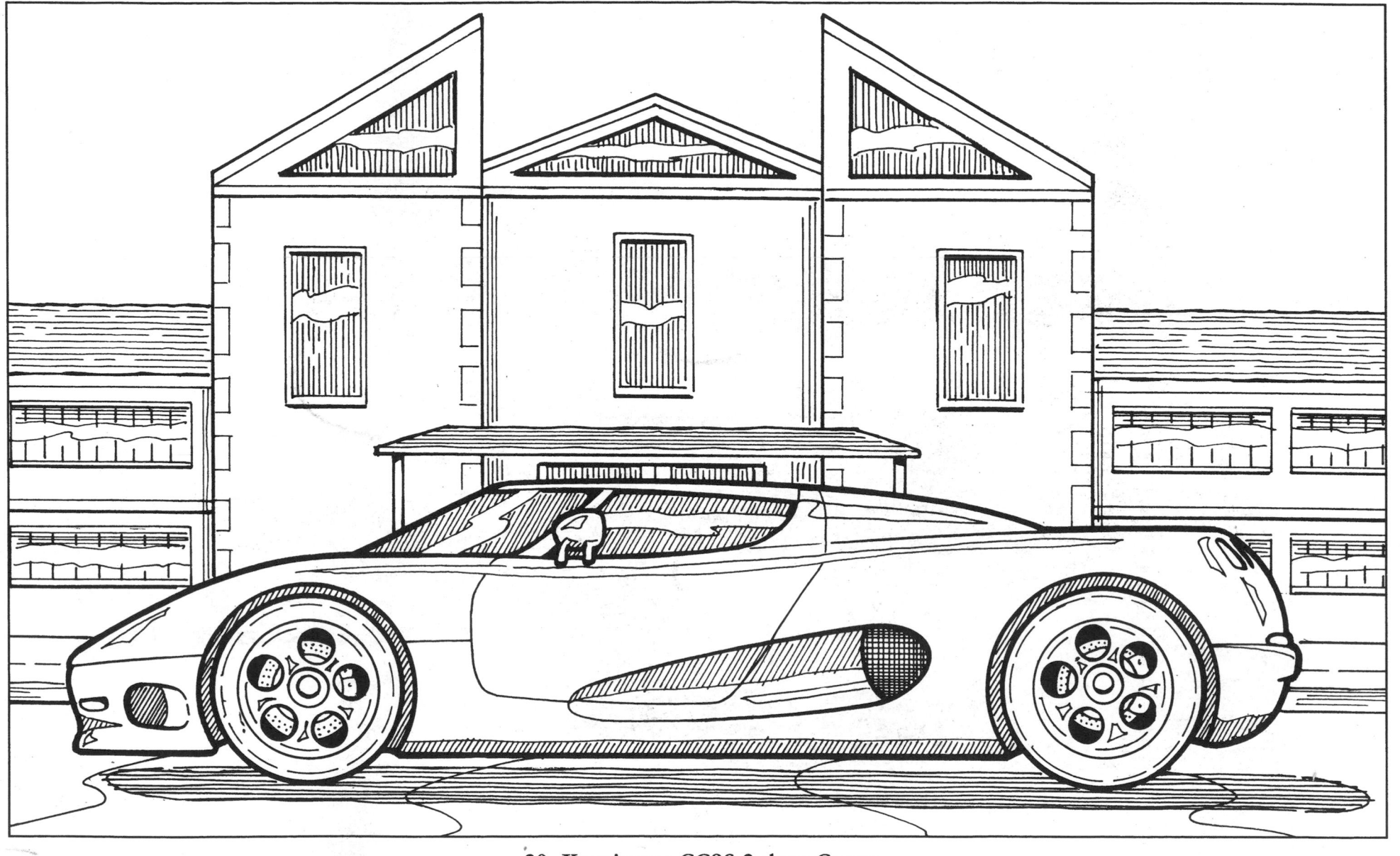

30. Koenigsegg CC8S 2-door Coupe
(World's Fastest Production Car: 242 mph)

Since its introduction in 2002, the Swedish-built Koenigsegg CC8S has held the prestigious title of "Fastest Production Car in the World." Its designer and builder, Christian Koenigsegg, set out to capture that crown, and did so with stunning success.

The CC8S has been officially clocked at a top speed of 242 mph. The powerplant for this world record-holder is a 4.6-liter Ford V-8 supercharged to produce a thumping 655 hp. This can propel the CC8S to 60 mph in a mere 3.3 seconds. Koenigsegg plans to produce only 20 CC8Ss per year.